**THE ROYAL COURT
THEATRE PRESENTS**

LELA & CO.

by Cordelia Lynn

Lela & Co. is part of the Royal Court's Jerwood New
Playwrights Programme, supported by the Jerwood
Charitable Foundation.

Lela & Co. was first performed at the Royal Court
Jerwood Theatre Upstairs, Sloane Square, on
Thursday 3 September 2015.

LELA & CO.

by Cordelia Lynn

CAST (in alphabetical order)

A Man **David Mumeni**
Lela **Katie West**

Director **Jude Christian**
Designer **Ana Inés Jabares-Pita**
Lighting Designer **Oliver Fenwick**
Sound Designer **David McSeveney**
Assistant Director **Rachel Nwokoro**
Casting Director **Amy Ball**
Production Manager **Lloyd Thomas for Jamie Hendry Productions**
Costume Supervisor **Lauren Butler**
Fight Director **Pamela Donald**
Dialect Coach **Helen Ashton**
Stage Managers **Nic Donithorn, Ellie Williams**
Stage Management Placement **Kinga Czynciel**
Set constructed and painted by **Ridiculous Solutions**

Conceived by
& developed with **Desara Bosnja & 1989 Productions**

The Royal Court & Stage Management wish to thank the following for their help with this production: McDougalls, Helen Murray, Richard Pinner, Lucy Sierra.

LELA & CO.
by Cordelia Lynn

Cordelia Lynn (Writer)

Cordelia Lynn is a writer whose debut play **After the War** has been performed in venues around the UK and abroad. Her second, **Believers Anonymous**, was staged at the Rosemary Branch Theatre in 2012 (Time Out Critic's Choice). She has taken part in the Royal Court Young Writers Programme in 2012 and is a member of the Soho Theatre Young Writers Company. She has recently completed an episode of the podcast sitcom **Wooden Overcoats**, produced by Audioscribble.

Jude Christian (Director)

As Director, theatre includes: **Split/Mixed** (Soho); **Harajuku Girls** (Finborough); **I'd Rather Goya Robbed Me Of My Sleep Than Some Other Son Of A Bitch** (Boom Arts, Portland); **How Do You Eat An Elephant/Bwyta Eliffant, Sut Mae Gwneud Hynny Dwedwch?** (National Youth Theatre of Wales); **Happy, The Mushroom** (Pentabus Young Writers' Festival); **Punk Rock, Last Easter** (RADA); **I'd Rather Goya Robbed Me of My Sleep than Some Other Arsehole** (Gate); **Balansera** (Poole Lighthouse); **Sonata Movements** (Blue Elephant); **My Romantic History** (English Theatre Berlin); **Bonfires** (The Miniaturists).

Opera includes: **©alculated to Death** (Tête-à-Tête Festival).

As Assistant Director, theatre includes: **Carmen Disruption** (Almeida); **Gone Fishing** (ROH Youth Opera Company); **The Prophet** (Gate); **Ein Mädchen namens Elvis** (Deutsches Theater Autorentheatertage).

Jude is Artistic Director of Concert Theatre and a Creative Associate at the Gate Theatre.

Oliver Fenwick (Lighting Designer)

For the Royal Court: **Routes, The Witness, Disconnect.**

Other theatre includes: **Love's Labour's Lost, Much Ado About Nothing, The Jew of Malta, Wendy & Peter Pan, The Winter's Tale, The Taming Of The Shrew, Julius Caesar, The Drunks, The Grain Store** (RSC); **The Motherf**ker With The Hat, The Holy Rosenburgs, The Passion, Happy Now?** (National); **The Vote, Berenice, Huis Clos** (Donmar); **My City, Ruined** (Almeida); **Multitudes, Red Velvet, Paper Dolls, Bracken Moor, Handbagged** (Tricycle); **Di & Viv & Rose, Handbagged, The Importance of Being Earnest, Bakersfield Mist, The Madness Of George III, Ghosts, Kean, The Solid Gold Cadillac,** **Secret Rapture** (West End); **The King's Speech** (tour); **After Miss Julie** (Young Vic); **Saved, A Midsummer Night's Dream** (Lyric, Hammersmith); **To Kill A Mockingbird, Hobson's Choice, The Beggars Opera** (Regent's Park Open Air); **Therese Raquin, The Big Meal, King Lear, Candida** (Theatre Royal, Bath); **Into The Woods, Sunday In the Park With George** (Chatelet, Paris); **The Kitchen Sink, The Contingency Plan, If There Is I Haven't Found It Yet** (Bush); **A Number, Travels With My Aunt** (Menier Chocolate Factory); **Private Lives, The Giant; Glass Eels; Comfort Me With Apples** (Hampstead); **Restoration** (Headlong); **Pride & Prejudice, Hamlet, The Caretaker, The Comedy of Errors, Bird Calls, Iphigenia** (Crucible, Sheffield).

Opera includes: **Werther** (Scottish Opera); **The Merry Widow** (Opera North/Sydney Opera House); **Samson et Delilah, Lohengrin, The Trojan Trilogy, The Nose, The Gentle Giant** (ROH).

Ana Inés Jabares-Pita (Designer)

As Designer, theatre includes: **The Driver's Seat** (National Theatre of Scotland); **The Echo Chamber** (Young Vic); **One Flea Spare, The Imposter** (Platform); **Hellscreen** (The Vaults Festival); **Domestica** (UK tour/Spain tour); **IDOMENEUS** (Gate); **The Legacy of Leadership** (Hilton Hotel, Blackpool); **As You Like It** (Rose, London); **Julius Caesar** (St Paul's Church, London); **The Freedom Plays** (Courtyard); **Hamlet's Fool** (Cockpit); **Sappho...9 Fragments** (UK tour/Canada tour).

As Designer, dance includes: **Histoire du soldat, Le carnaval des animaux, Pierino e il Lupo** (TeatroPoliteama, Palermo).

As Assistant Designer, theatre includes: **The Birthday Party** (Royal Exchange, Manchester); **Hamlet** (The Shakespeare Garden, Paris); **Der Zigeunerbaron** (Stadttheater Klagenfurt).

As Assistant Designer, opera includes: **La Celestina** (Metropolitan Museum of New York); **Jacob Lenz** (ENO); **The Turn of the Screw** (Northern Ireland Opera); **I Capuleti e i Montecchi** (Teatro Sociale Como); **Toujours et Pres de Moi** (Hoxton Hall).

As Scenic Artist, opera includes: **Die Gezeneichten, La fanciulla del West** (Teatro Massimo, Palermo).

Awards include: **The Linbury Prize for Stage Design, Fringe Theatre Festival Ottawa Best Design Award.**

David McSeveney (Sound Designer)

For the Royal Court: **Constellations (& West End/ Broadway/tour), Teh Internet is Serious Business, The Art of Dying, Not I/Footfalls/ Rockaby (& West End/National tour/ International tour), The Djinns of Eidgah, Routes, If You Don't Let Us Dream We Won't Let You Sleep, Belong, Vera Vera Vera, The Village Bike, Clybourne Park (& West End), Ingredient X, Posh (& West End), Disconnect, Cock, A Miracle, The Stone, Shades, 7 Jewish Children, The Girlfriend Experience (& Theatre Royal, Plymouth/Young Vic), Contractions, Fear & Misery/War & Peace.**

Other theatre includes: **The Skriker (Manchester International Festival/Royal Exchange, Manchester); Blurred Lines (National); The Changeling (Young Vic); A Doll's House (Young Vic/West End/Brooklyn Academy of Music, New York); The Duke in Darkness (Tabard); The Winter's Tale (RSC); Stones in His Pockets (Tricycle); Victoria Station/ One for the Road (Print Room/Young Vic); On The Record (Arcola); The Tin Horizon (503); Gaslight (Old Vic); Charley's Aunt, An Hour & a Half Late (Theatre Royal, Bath); A Passage to India, After Mrs Rochester, Madame Bovary (Shared Experience); Men Should Weep, Rookery Nook (Oxford Stage Company); Othello (Southwark Playhouse).**

David is Head of Sound at the Royal Court.

David Mumeni (A Man)

Theatre includes: **True Brits (HighTide); Mush & Me (Bush/Underbelly, Edinburgh); The Machine (Donmar/Manchester International Festival/Park Avenue Armory, New York); 'Tis Pity She's a Whore (Cheek by Jowl/Barbican/ International tour); The TS Elliot US/UK Exchange (Vineyard, New York/Old Vic).**

Television includes: **Finding Jesus, Phoneshop, Cuckoo, Confessions from the Underground, Fresh Meat, Doctors, Whitechapel.**

Film includes: **The Huntsman, Noble, The Inbetweeners Movie.**

Rachel Nwokoro (Assistant Director)

As Assistant Director, theatre includes: **The Ice Break (Birmingham Opera Company); Hamlet (Lion & Unicorn).**

As Performer, theatre includes: **Testimonial to All Women Who Fall Short of Perfection (The Shadows Are Talking); At the Stroke of Midnight (Etcetera); Arcadia (Hild Bede); The Government Inspector (Assembly Rooms); On the Spot - The Jemima Kyle Show, Yard Gal (Soho); The Witches of Eastwick (West End); Bridge Night (Tristan Bates); It's Real on Road (Youth Inc); Luna Club (Lyric, Hammersmith).**

Lloyd Thomas for Jamie Hendry Productions (Production Manager)

Theatre includes: **The Mentalists, Impossible, Constellations, Let It Be, A View From a Bridge, Neville's Island, Uncle Vanya (West End).**

Katie West (Lela)

Theatre includes: **Carmen Disruption (Almeida); Hamlet, Blinded-Sided, Blithe Spirit (Royal Exchange, Manchester); Macbeth (Manchester International Festival); The Thrill of Love (New Vic); A Taste of Honey (Crucible, Sheffield); 65 Miles, Once Upon a Time in Wigan (Hull Truck); Glory Dazed (Underbelly); Vote of No Confidence (503); Punk Rock (Lyric, Hammersmith); Sense (Southwark); Manchester (Contact).**

Television includes: **Doctors, Without You, United.**

Film includes: **Cinderella.**

JERWOOD CHARITABLE FOUNDATION

Jerwood New Playwrights is a longstanding partnership between Jerwood Charitable Foundation and the Royal Court. 2015 is the 21st anniversary of the programme which supports the production of three new works by emerging writers, all of whom are in the first 10 years of their career.

The Royal Court carefully identifies playwrights whose careers would benefit from the challenge and profile of being fully produced either in the Jerwood Downstairs or Jerwood Upstairs Theatres at the Royal Court.

Since 1994, the programme has produced a collection of challenging and outspoken works which explore a variety of new forms and voices and so far has supported the production of 77 new plays. These plays include: Joe Penhall's **Some Voices**, Nick Grosso's **Peaches** and **Real Classy Affair**, Judy Upton's **Ashes and Sand**, Sarah Kane's **Blasted, Cleansed** and **4.48 Psychosis**, Michael Wynne's **The Knocky** and **The People are Friendly**, Judith Johnson's **Uganda**, Sebastian Barry's **The Steward of Christendom**, Jez Butterworth's **Mojo**, Mark Ravenhill's **Shopping and Fucking**, Ayub Khan Din's **East is East** and **Notes on Falling Leaves**, Martin McDonagh's **The Beauty Queen of Leenane**, Jess Walters' **Cockroach, Who?**, Tamantha Hammerschlag's **Backpay**, Connor McPherson's **The Weir**, Meredith Oakes' **Faith**, Rebecca Prichard's **Fair Game**, Roy Williams' **Lift Off, Clubland** and **Fallout**, Richard Bean's **Toast** and **Under the Whaleback**, Gary Mitchell's **Trust** and **The Force of Change**, Mick Mahoney's **Sacred Heart** and **Food Chain**, Marina Carr's **On Raftery's Hill**, David Eldridge's **Under the Blue Sky** and **Incomplete and Random Acts of Kindness**, David Harower's **Presence**, Simon Stephens' **Herons, Country Music** and **Motortown**, Leo Butler's **Redundant** and **Lucky Dog**, Enda Walsh's **Bedbound**, David Greig's **Outlying Islands**, Zinnie Harris' **Nightingale and Chase**, Grae Cleugh's **Fucking Games**, Rona Munro's **Iron**, Ché Walker's **Fleshwound**, Laura Wade's **Breathing Corpses**, debbie tucker green's **Stoning Mary**, Gregory Burke's **On Tour**, Stella Feehily's **O Go My Man**, Simon Faquhar's **Rainbow Kiss**, April de Angelis, Stella Feehily, Tanika Gupta, Chloe Moss and Laura Wade's **Catch**, Polly Stenham's **That Face** and **Tusk Tusk**, Mike Bartlett's **My Child**, Fiona Evans' **Scarborough**, Levi David Addai's **Oxford Street**, Bola Agbaje's **Gone Too Far!** and **Off The Endz**, Alexi Kaye Campbell's **The Pride**, Alia Bano's **Shades**, Tim Crouch's **The Author**, DC Moore's **The Empire**, Anya Reiss' **Spur of the Moment** and **The Acid Test**, Penelope Skinner's **The Village Bike**, Rachel De-lahay's **The Westbridge** and **Routes**, Nick Payne's **Constellations**, Vivienne Franzmann's **The Witness** and **Pests**, E. V. Crowe's **Hero**, Anders Lustgarten's **If You Don't Let Us Dream, We Won't Let You Sleep**, Suhayla El-Bushra's **Pigeons**, Clare Lizzimore's **Mint**, Alistair McDowall's **Talk Show**, Rory Mullarkey's **The Wolf From The Door**, Molly Davies' **God Bless The Child** and Diana Nneka Atuona's **Liberian Girl**.

Jerwood Charitable Foundation is dedicated to imaginative and responsible revenue funding of the arts, supporting artists to develop and grow at important stages in their careers. It works with artists across art forms, from dance and theatre to literature, music and the visual arts.

jerwoodcharitablefoundation.org

THE ROYAL COURT THEATRE

The Royal Court Theatre is the writers' theatre. It is the leading force in world theatre for energetically cultivating writers – undiscovered, new, and established.

Through the writers the Royal Court is at the forefront of creating restless, alert, provocative theatre about now, inspiring audiences and influencing future writers. Through the writers the Royal Court strives to constantly reinvent the theatre ecology, creating theatre for everyone.

We invite and enable conversation and debate, allowing writers and their ideas to reach and resonate beyond the stage, and the public to share in the thinking.

Over 120,000 people visit the Royal Court in Sloane Square, London, each year and many thousands more see our work elsewhere through transfers to the West End and New York, national and international tours, residencies across London and site-specific work.

The Royal Court's extensive development activity encompasses a diverse range of writers and artists and includes an ongoing programme of writers' attachments, readings, workshops and playwriting groups. Twenty years of pioneering work around the world means the Royal Court has relationships with writers on every continent.

The Royal Court opens its doors to radical thinking and provocative discussion, and to the unheard voices and free thinkers that, through their writing, change our way of seeing.

Within the past sixty years, John Osborne, Arnold Wesker and Howard Brenton have all started their careers at the Court. Many others, including Caryl Churchill, Mark Ravenhill and Sarah Kane have followed. More recently, the theatre has found and fostered new writers such as Polly Stenham, Mike Bartlett, Bola Agbaje, Nick Payne and Rachel De-lahay and produced many iconic plays from Laura Wade's **Posh** to Bruce Norris' **Clybourne Park** and Jez Butterworth's **Jerusalem**. Royal Court plays from every decade are now performed on stage and taught in classrooms across the globe.

It is because of this commitment to the writer that we believe there is no more important theatre in the world than the Royal Court.

Supported using public funding by

ARTS COUNCIL ENGLAND

NEW SEASON
SEP 2015 - JAN 2016

JERWOOD THEATRE
DOWNSTAIRS

10 Sep – 10 Oct
Hangmen
By Martin McDonagh
Directed by Matthew Dunster

In his small pub in Oldham, Harry is something of a local celebrity. But what's the second-best hangman in England to do on the day they've abolished hanging?

21 Oct - 14 Nov
RoosevElvis
Created by the TEAM
Directed by Rachel Chavkin

A new work about gender, appetite, and the multitudes we contain.

RoosevElvis at the Royal Court is supported by The Andrew W. Mellon Foundation.

25 Nov - 9 Jan
Linda
By Penelope Skinner
Directed by Michael Longhurst

At 55, Linda seems to have it all. But she isn't satisfied. Beneath the surface, the cracks are starting to show.

JERWOOD THEATRE
UPSTAIRS

14 Oct - 21 Nov
Plaques and Tangles
By Nicola Wilson
Directed by Lucy Morrison

Suffering with early onset Alzheimer's, Megan lurches through time on a wild memory trip while her young family deal with the consequences.

3 Dec - 9 Jan
You For Me For You
By Mia Chung
Directed by Richard Twyman

North Korean sisters Minhee and Junhee attempt to flee the Best Nation in the World.

020 7565 5000 (no booking fee)
royalcourttheatre.com

Follow us 🐦 royalcourt 📘 royalcourttheatre
Royal Court Theatre Sloane Square London, SW1W 8AS

Plaques and Tangles is part of the Royal Court's Jerwood New Playwrights programme, supported by Jerwood Charitable Foundation.

Innovation partner

 ARTS COUNCIL ENGLAND

JERWOOD CHARITABLE FOUNDATION

ROYAL COURT SUPPORTERS

The Royal Court is a registered charity and not–for–profit company. We need to raise £1.7 million every year in addition to our core grant from the Arts Council and our ticket income to achieve what we do.

We have significant and longstanding relationships with many generous organisations and individuals who provide vital support. Royal Court supporters enable us to remain the writers' theatre, find stories from everywhere and create theatre for everyone.

We can't do it without you.

Innovation partner

Supported using public funding by
ARTS COUNCIL ENGLAND

EMPLOYEES
THE ROYAL COURT & ENGLISH STAGE COMPANY

Royal Court Theatre
Sloane Square,
London SW1W 8AS
Tel: 020 7565 5050
info@royalcourttheatre.com
www.royalcourttheatre.com

Artistic Director
Vicky Featherstone
Executive Producer
Lucy Davies

Associate Directors
**Lucy Morrison,
Hamish Pirie, John
Tiffany**
Associate Designer
Chloe Lamford
Associate Playwright
Simon Stephens
Associate Artists
**Carrie Cracknell,
Simon Godwin,
Katie Mitchell**

Artistic Associate
Ola Animashawun
Trainee Director
Roy Alexander Weise‡

International Director
Elyse Dodgson
Associate Director
(International)
Richard Twyman
International Assistant
Sarah Murray

Head of Young Court
Lynne Gagliano*
Deputy Head of Young
Court **Romana Flello**
Young Court Apprentice
Maia Clarke

Literary Manager
**Christopher
Campbell**
Deputy Literary Manager
Louise Stephens
Literary Administrator
Hayley Dallimore
Trainee Administrator
(Literary)
Ashiokai Omaboe§

Head of Casting
Amy Ball
Casting Assistant
Arthur Carrington

Head of Production
Matt Noddings
Head of Lighting
Jack Williams
Deputy Head of Lighting
Marec Joyce

Lighting Technicians
**Jess Faulks,
Matthew Harding**
Head of Stage
Steven Stickler
Stage Deputy
Dan Lockett
Stage Chargehand
Lee Crimmen
Chargehand & Building
Maintenance Technician
Matt Livesey
Head of Sound
David McSeveney
Sound Deputy
Emily Legg
Sound Operator
**Madison English,
Laura Hammond**
Technical Trainee
Ashley Lednor§
Head of Costume
Lucy Walshaw
Wardrobe Manager
Gina Lee

General Manager
**Catherine
Thornborrow**
Assistant Producer
Minna Sharpe
Projects Producer
Chris James
Assistant to the Executive
Ryan Govin
Trainee Administrator
(Producing)
Cherrelle Glave§
Associate Producer
(Tottenham & Pimlico)
Daniel Brodie*
Community Producer
(Tottenham & Pimlico)
Chris Sonnex*

Finance Director
Helen Perryer
Financial Controller
Morris MacDonagh
Financial Administrator
Rosie Mortimer

Head of Press & Publicity
Anoushka Hay

Head of Marketing
& Sales
Becky Wootton
Deputy Head of Marketing
Holly Conneely
Marketing Manager
Dion Wilson
Communications Trainees
**Katie Davison§, Rida
Hamidou§**

Sales Manager
Liam Geoghegan
Deputy Sales Manager
Helen Corbett
Box Office Sales
Assistants
**Laura Duncanson,
Joe Hodgson, Helen
Preddy*, Margaret
Perry***

Head of Development
Rebecca Kendall
Deputy Head of
Development
Lucy Buxton
Senior Individual Giving
Manager
Sue Livermore*
Trusts & Foundations
Manager
Clare O'Hara*
Development Managers
**Luciana Lawlor, Anna
Sampson**
Development Officer
Nadia Vistisen

Theatre Manager **Rachel
Dudley**
Senior Duty House
Manager
Adam Lawler
Venue Operations
Apprentice
Naomi Wright
Duty House Managers
**Florence Bourne,
Elinor Keber, Tanya
Shields**
Caretaker
Christian Rudolph
Bar & Kitchen Manager
Ali Christian
Deputy Bar &
Kitchen Manager
Robert Smael
Assistant Bar &
Kitchen Manager
Jared Thomas
Head Chef
Tim Jenner
Sous Chef
Mandy Fitzhugh
Bookshop Manager
Simon David
Bookshop Assistant
Vanessa Hammick*

Stage Door/Reception
**Paul Lovegrove,
Tyrone Lucas,
Jane Wainwright**

Thanks to all of our Ushers
and Bar & Kitchen staff.

§ Posts supported by
The Sackler Trust
Trainee Scheme
‡The post of Trainee
Director is supported
by an anonymous donor.
* Part-time.

Remember the Royal Court in your will and help to ensure that our future is as iconic as our past.

Every gift, whatever the amount, will help us maintain and care for the building, support the next generation of playwrights starting out in their career, deliver our education programme and put our plays on the stage.

LEAVE A LEGACY

To discuss leaving a legacy to the Royal Court, please contact:

Sue Livermore, Senior Individual Giving Manager,
Royal Court Theatre, Sloane Square,
London, SW1W 8AS

Email: suelivermore@royalcourttheatre.com
Tel: 020 7565 5079

LOVE NEW WRITING

LELA & CO.

a monologue

Cordelia Lynn

Characters

LELA
A MAN
FATHER, *Lela's father*
JAY, *Lela's brother-in-law*
HUSBAND, *a businessman*
PEACEKEEPER, *a soldier*

Notes

All male parts to be played by the same actor.

/ indicates an interruption and, where appropriate, the place of interruption within a sentence.

This text went to press before the end of rehearsals and so may differ slightly from the play as performed.

Lights up.

LELA *and* A MAN *onstage.*

LELA. When I was born the women greeted me with singing.
   Not my mother, obviously, she was flat out on her back like a
   felled tree, which seems fair enough given the circumstances,
   but my grandmother sang me to sleep that first time, and the
   maiden aunts did their bit till my mother was back to herself
   again and could join in the task of lullabying. That's a
   woman's responsibility, see? And when my grandmother died
   my mother and the aunts sang her into oblivion because that's
   a woman's responsibility too, to sing the songs, the early
   songs and the late songs, the songs of sleeping and the songs
   of mourning. That's how it works here, women wake you up
   and they put you to sleep, they bring you into life and then
   they ease you into death. Men handle the bits in between.
   (*Beat.*) It was a hard birth, and outside a storm was raging, and
   while my mother struggled me into life and I myself struggled
   my way out of the dark, the land struggled with the sky and
   vice versa, wind and rain and rage, and the aunts said that I
   was a storm child, a storm-born child, and that that meant
   something – though just what it meant they kept mum on – but
   despite the struggle I was born healthy and whole and raring
   to go, and my mother, though she was well and truly felled for
   a good week after, was healthy and whole too in the end, and
   that, as they say, was that. (*Beat.*) Speaking of felling, I've
   seen a great deal of it in my time. I've seen trees felled, sure,
   wind and chainsaws, you name it, but I've seen buildings
   felled too, cranes, bombs, fire and mines. I've seen a whole
   city felled. I've seen people felled, men and women. And
   children. But that came later. (*Beat.*) I come from the
   mountains. It's a nice enough place, if you're partial to a
   landscape, which I am. You have to be partial to a landscape,
   if you're not, well there's not much else to be partial to. Sheep,
   I suppose, but the less said of that the better. Up in the
   mountains the north wind blows, and the north-east, battling it
   out for supremacy over the uplands; I'm partial to a windscape

too, like I can see it, see the swell like the swell on water, the chaotic eddies, the ripple effect when it crosses over and above itself, how I see it when it ripples the lake. This much I know, I could (and I have, as you'll soon hear) walk a hundred miles in each direction and my skin would still be dominated by the north-north-easterly winds. So there's comfort in that.

Pause.

(*Singing.*) 'Oh Western Wind, when wilt / thou blow…'

A MAN (*taking over, singing*). 'Thou blow…'

Pause.

LELA. Other than when she was flat on her back, circumstances dictating that position, and me being the last of the circumstances, my mother wasn't anything like a tree. She was small and sprightly, *petite* (that's French), bones like husks of straw, my grandmother too, and my aunts. That's what the women in our family are like, bird-like; twitchy, my father says. I'm the same, and my sister Em, but not my sister Elle who's different, she's got curves like a *river*, I kid you not. Pleased as a peach about it too, always twisting about in front of the mirror, shoving her boobs up and together with her hands, you know, not that they needed it, talking rubbish that she was a real woman – whatever that is – and me and Em being pretty jealous despite ourselves, us being like sticks, although a man once told me I had a waist like a wand. Like a *wand*. That's what he said. (*Beat.*) Anyway, we got a bit sick of all the 'Oo look at me I'm Marilyn Monroe', Em and I did, and so we started teasing her saying she was like that because Father wasn't actually her father but she was in truth the love child of Zed, who's the fat man that ran the petrol pump. Elle didn't like that at all, not one bit, even though it didn't actually make sense because we got it, the sprightliness, from Mother anyway not Father, but we weren't really thinking about the intricacies of genetics at the time, I can tell you. So we're singing 'Fatty fatty boom boom fatty fatty boom boom you're Zed's fat sperm child' and Elle goes running off to Father sobbing and telling tales and he beat me and Em and said we were dishonouring our mother and so we were dishonouring him and he won't be dishonoured by his own daughters under his own never-anything-but-honourable roof, and that is a

sight to see, I can tell you, the two of us running screaming
round the kitchen table, and Father running after us shouting
dishonour and clobbering us when he can get a handhold, and
Mother screaming too because even though she wasn't too
keen on the implication that she'd had a quickie behind the
petrol pump with fat Zed all of thirteen years ago, she still
didn't like the beatings, and of course the aunts were
screaming, because why not?, and Grandma was screaming
too because that's the thing to do in those situations, as well
she knew, sixty-five at the time if she were a day, and then Elle
got the same idea and so she was screaming and running after
us and Father's shouting blue murder: 'Dishonour this and
dishonour that', and beating her too at the end of it because
that's just what happens if you start a scene in a house full of
women and just one man but he's the one with the fists. (*Beat*.)
But it's not like we couldn't make him suffer for it afterwards,
not one of us looking him in the eye for weeks and making
him invisible when he comes into the room and shutting up
whatever it was we were saying and he stomps around for a bit
then leaves with his tail between his legs (in more ways than
one, if you see what I mean), and there's nothing quite like
being made invisible by a house full of women, I can tell you,
so one day he comes home with a big box of chocolates for us
girls, foreign ones, the best ones, and that was the end of it,
because he was a good man really, our father, and I think that
sometimes he just needed to remind himself that he existed.
(*Beat*.) And to tell the truth, if there's one thing I learnt the
hard way, later on, and I'll give you this for free, it's don't
scream like that, whatever they do, don't scream like that on
your life, no not on your *life* /

FATHER. Lela!

LELA. It sets something going in them, it really does, I reckon
it's something biological, that there's a certain pitch in a
woman's scream and it sends them crazy /

FATHER. Lela!

LELA. Like with babies screaming how it can drive you crazy,
and they see red and that's the fact of / the matter...

FATHER. Where's that girl, I swear to God I'll beat her black
and blue when I get my hands on her – Lela!

LELA. Yes Dad!

FATHER. Don't 'Yes Dad' me shouting in the house like a
tramp come here this moment or I'll beat you till your arse
drops off you disgusting child!

LELA. You swear to God you'll beat me black and blue when
you get your hands on me, and you swear you'll beat me if
you don't, so what do you think I am, stupid?

*He chases her round the house, catches her and beats her.
She wails.*

FATHER (*beating her relentlessly*). What did I do to deserve
this, oh God, what did I do in a previous life to deserve this
existence trapped in a house filled with screaming, scheming,
cake-eating women!

LELA. Mummeeeeeeeeyy!!!! (*Etc.*)

FATHER. Oh God, I work myself to death buying treats and
presents for my little girls and how do they repay me, how
do they repay me, Lela? They eat the cake I've slaved for,
a week's wages for one special cake, the greatest cake our
village has ever seen, the messiah of birthday cakes, and
she eats the cake, my God, she eats the cake like a thief in
the night!

LELA. It wasn't meeeeeeeee... (*Etc.*)

FATHER. The most ungrateful of daughters! Oh Lord, what have
I done to deserve this most ungrateful of all children! This
merciless, cake-guzzling, father-into-an-early-graving brat!

Beat.

LELA. That was about the cake, see? My thirteenth birthday
cake. Because, and I don't want you to get the wrong idea,
despite the beatings and the shoutings and the what-have-I-
done-to-deserve-this-ings, my father loved us and spoilt us
rotten, and he was proud as you please when his youngest
daughter turned thirteen and there he is with his three lovely
girls, all women now, though two as skinny as sticks including
yours truly, and I hadn't – but he wasn't to know this – started
bleeding yet because we were all late, the women in my
family, except for, predictably, 'I'm-a-real-woman' Elle who

came on like a burst pipe at twelve and bled to the clock every
month like a gutted pig, strewn across the bed with her hand
on her brow – just so – moaning and writhing and having the
aunts bring her sweet tea all hours of the day and night. (*Beat*.)
But to get back to the point, Father decided we were going to
have a special party just for me on my thirteenth birthday, and
we'd set up tables in the garden and Mother had borrowed
white tablecloths and extra chairs, and scrubbed everything till
you could have eaten off the floor (though why you'd want to
do that I don't know because we'd borrowed extra dishes and
cutlery too), and the aunts sat at the kitchen table for a week
shelling peas and beans and skinning vegetables like there was
no tomorrow, and we had to excavate Grandma from the pods
and peel (she'd been missing for two days before we realised
what had happened), and we were inviting all the children
from my school, and Father's friends were coming and their
wives who were Mother's friends and the four surviving old
hens and one surviving old cock who were Grandma's friends
and even the aunts' maiden-aunt friends (because maiden
aunts keep to their own, as any fool knows), and Father had
ordered specially from the baker in the town, like he said, the
messiah of all birthday cakes. And that was a sight to see too
when he brought it back in the little car, sat in the passenger
seat like he'd brought home a new bride, all done up in a
white box with baby-blue ribbons and *Pâtisserie Française*
written on it in swirly writing (that's French for French
Patisserie which is how you knew it was posh), and, my, how
we gathered round when, with shaking hands, he undid the
ribbons and opened the box to reveal this giant paradise of
pink icing, a cake the size and intricacy of a palace all frosted
in an inch thick of pink sugar with 'Happy Birthday Little
Lela' printed on it in white in the same swirly writing as on the
box and parapets and arabesques of white icing all around the
edge. (*Beat*.) Now that was a sight to see. (*Beat*.) That very
night, the night before the party, someone snuck down into the
kitchen and tiptoed past Grandma, who even slept in there in
her chair by the stove, was born, in fact, in that room sixty-
eight years before and died in there too when she was seventy
(which was when her mother died and her mother before her
and her mother before her), and when her father and uncles
and brothers were all killed during the rebellions, like so many

men in the uplands, she and her mother stayed in that house, and so you could say she'd spent most of her life in that kitchen because I don't once remember seeing her out of it, and towards the end of her time not even out of that chair. (*Beat*.) Though, living as long as she did, we had our suspicions she crept out into the garden in the middle of the night and did yoga under the stars because she'd read in a magazine once about Indian Brahmins who lived to a hundred and hadn't eaten even a grain of rice since they were twenty /

FATHER. Your grandmother, God keep her soul, did *not* sneak out into the garden at night to do yoga!

Beat.

LELA. Well, *I* had *my* suspicions that /

FATHER. God rest your grandmother's soul she did *not* sneak anywhere not ever in her life did she sneak, not even to do yoga, rice-eating Brahmin or no rice-eating Brahmin, and that's the end of the matter.

Beat.

LELA. Well anyway, the fact is, normally you couldn't have put a thing past Grandma but she was still recovering from her ordeal of being buried alive under vegetable peelings for two days, and so that person, whoever it was, snuck right round her and took one of Mother's knives – that Father was wont to brandish at her while demanding what had he ever done to deserve such an existence et cetera et cetera – and that person made a little incision in the pink casing of the cake, and peeled off an inch-thick flap of pink skin and, it has always been assumed, ate it. (*Beat*.) My bet has always been Elle. She had a sweet tooth, she would have had to to keep those curves happy and fed, but no matter my protestations over the years, to this very day, it has become family legend how, on the eve of my thirteenth birthday, I desecrated the messiah of birthday cakes, greedy ungrateful girl that I was, and my father tells the story again and again, there's not a person in our village doesn't know the story, and my second husband now, he tells the story too, of an evening; it's a story well told, though a lie, but a story that has become truth in the telling. But speaking of lies and truth, this that I tell you now, what you have come here to listen to, this, all this, is the whole truth and nothing but, I swear it on my little son's life and on my little girl's death: this is the true story of Lela, yours truly, in truth, forever and ever – amen.

Pause.

(*Singing.*) 'Oh Western Wind, when wilt thou / blow? The small...'

A MAN (*taking over, singing*). 'Blow? The small rain...'

Pause.

LELA. Well. So much for childhood. Em got married first, being the eldest and five years my senior. Nice fellow, strong hands – which is a good sign in a man, so say the aunts, and it's the privilege of women who've never married themselves to know the good and bad signs in a man, and at that, the good and bad in a man, and to dispense advice, approval or doom and gloom, as the mood takes them – they've got perspective, see? Then it was Elle's turn, not long after the fiasco with the cake, and you can imagine she'd been having enough fun without it, with every man in a ten-mile radius queueing up, and she said that men needed someone like her, what with all the violence and the fighting there was around this time, she said they'd want a 'real woman' to comfort them at night, men not being comforted, as she was pleased to let me know, by skinny shanks such as myself with hip bones that could break a doorknob should you collide. (*Beat.*) Though that's not a true story either, for the record. And in the end she settled for Jay, who hadn't actually seen much fighting anyway, it was true, but was a real scoop with his university education, and knowing about business and things, and working in the city by the sea with the foreign people who had come to sort out our country. (*Beat.*) Funny how it turns out but I could teach Elle a thing or two about comforting men in the night, now all's said and done. If that's what you call comfort. But in my family, these days, there are things that are not said, and they've reason enough as you'll soon hear because /

JAY. Now little Lela had a little crush on me, her sister's husband as I was /

LELA. I didn't have a crush on him /

JAY. And I couldn't blame her of course, because what can you expect of a thirteen-year-old girl, innocent as the day she was born /

LELA. I *don't* have a crush on you, I /

JAY. And as a man, such as myself, you take that as it comes, as, indeed, a compliment from a sweet little thing and – above all – you treat it with respect, and her with respect too, being the little sister of my dear wife, Elle, the dearest, most charming wife a man ever had and *not* – if you don't mind my saying – lacking in the sack department, ha ha. But, I put it to you: how is a little girl, such as our little Lela, supposed to navigate her way – that's right, I use the word advisedly – navigate her way through the minefield of socio-sexual exchange and intercourse (in both senses of the word – ha ha). Little girls, we know, are trusting, but little girls are also curious: a devastating combination. For what did curiosity kill, Lela? (*Tiny beat.*) What did curiosity kill, Lela?

LELA. The cat.

JAY. Quite right Lela, the cat, or should we say kitten – ha ha ha! Get it? (*Beat.*) Anyway, as I was saying, what's a girl to do? She wants to play the game, fair enough in my opinion, and quite right too, but how is she supposed to play the game safely and well, avoid the card-sharks so to speak, if she doesn't have any practice in the game? You take my point, yes? Which is exactly why I, as her brother-in-law, husband to her dear and very delightful sister Elle, am perfectly happy for her to have her little crush /

LELA. I don't /

JAY. To have her little crush and, indeed, to flex her flirting muscles, to exercise the strength of her sexual imagination, on me, where it's safe to do so. She loves sitting in my lap, don't you Lela? Yes, many's the time she'd come running and sit on my lap and look up with her big eyes and giggle at my jokes and wriggle about /

LELA. I /

JAY. Come along Lela, come and say hello to your brother.

He pulls her onto his lap.

LELA. Hello.

JAY. Have you been working hard at school?

LELA. Today we learnt that the economic value of a labour service is determined by the total amount of labour required to produce it.

JAY. That's very good Lela.

LELA. I want to go to university like you when I'm older.

JAY. And what would you like to study?

LELA. I like geography.

JAY. What? Colouring-in? Ha ha!

LELA. I want to learn about rocks and mountains, and how the weather works, and where the tides and the winds came from, and how the land was made.

JAY. I think that's very good, Lela. Here! Look what I've got for you... (*Produces, magic trick, a lollipop.*) Eat it, go on eat it.

LELA (*unwraps the lollipop. Looks at it*).

JAY. You have to suck it.

Beat.

LELA (*sucks the lollipop*).

He watches.

JAY (*beat*). So you see? Safe and wholesome, like a bird in a nest, where nothing can turn around and bite her on the behind, no sharks here, no. Though I don't want you to walk away with any misconceptions: a good and respectful brother-in-law I may be, but not a sap of a man, oh no, all man, me, and delighted too, as any man would be, at the kittenesque attentions and ministrations of my little sister-in-law, my little Lela; so no, though no shark, perhaps just a touch of the piraña – ha ha /

LELA. Pirañas are all jaw, except for a tiny tail, all jaw for their teeth.

JAY (*beat*).

LELA. I saw it in a picture book.

Beat.

JAY. She always had a wild imagination, that Lela.

LELA. They were good to me, Elle and her husband. I visited them in the city by the sea where he worked with the foreign people, and did good business and made good money, and she brought me books and nice clothes and things when she came home. It was as though, over that year, we suddenly came to understand each other, that, actually, however it was we expressed it, what we were both expressing was a yearning. (*Beat.*) All the same though, she was still ever so 'Look at me, I'm Elle sitting in a posh café in my mighty tight bright-red two-piece ladies' suit and golden-era-of-Hollywood lipstick sipping my espresso from a teensy tiny cup and eye-stabbing men over the rims of my fake designer sunglasses.' (*Beat.*) But if there's one thing you could say about Elle, amongst all the other things, it's that she knew where she was going and she knew what she wanted, and that was where she went and that was what she got, and there wasn't anything, not anything, that was going to stand in her way.

Pause.

I met my first husband in the city by the sea. I was there with Elle and Jay for a weekend to go swimming and sunbathe and drink nice drinks, the whole shebang, and I was having just the loveliest time; I'd bought a two-piece bikini costume especially for the occasion, so was feeling pretty pleased with myself, though I have to admit that the cloth sagged a little round the breasts and bum-like when I was in the water, but still, I was having a whale of a time. And I love that city, the buildings are so white, and so are the sands, and, oh it's a lovely hot temperature with everything blazing white white white – such a change from the breeze and the sudden chill in the mountains, and the damp and the rain on the air and the north-north-easterly wind, though that's what I love most of all to return to, as I one day did – and there's always a scent of lemons and olives, and the silver-leaved olive trees, and this carried on the sea-salty air, and I think it's one of the nicest scents and airs I've ever come across. Though these days I can't smell lemon without feeling sick. (*Beat.*) And then, it turned out, by chance, that Jay's friend from university – or was it his business acquaintance? – was also in the city that weekend, just happened to be there, and Jay bumped into him one night walking back from a bar, or something, so of course they decided we should meet and have a drink, and we met in the main city square which was this great big /

HUSBAND. It was on the beach.

Long beat: she puts her hands to her head.

LELA. So we met in the main city square and had a drink – and I guess they decided I was old enough to drink alcohol by that time and /

HUSBAND. It was on the beach.

LELA. There was a café in the square where I particularly liked to sit in the evenings, with chairs outside /

HUSBAND. It was on the beach. I met my wife, Lela, on the beach. She was holidaying with her sister and brother-in-law, an associate of mine. Myself, I come from over the border, but was in town seeing to some business matters. We arranged to meet on the beach, a beach bar /

LELA. It was in the city in the main square with the old cobbles /

HUSBAND. Where they served sweet sickly cocktails, the sort that women drink, and chilled beer, which is good in the heat /

LELA. It was /

HUSBAND. Yes. I think there is something very appealing about a nice chilled beer at the end of a hot day on the beach /

LELA. I had a glass of wine that Jay chose, knowing, as he did, about these things /

HUSBAND. Lela drank a cocktail, pink and sugary /

LELA. I hate cocktails /

HUSBAND. With a name like Sex Bomb or Screaming Orgasm, and a little cocktail umbrella /

LELA. I was shy of him, he seemed very distinguished, in his suit with his little trimmed moustache, a quiet sort of man with a very steady gaze, and nearly ten years my senior /

HUSBAND. She was a little flirt even then, barely fifteen years old, making eyes at me over her pink drink /

LELA. I'd catch him looking at me, very steady /

HUSBAND. And giggling loudly with her fat sister /

LELA. And it made me shudder inside, when I caught him looking at me /

HUSBAND. I've never liked my women fat, but each to their own /

LELA. A funny little shudder that was like something dropping out of me, an emptiness forming all of a sudden deep inside /

HUSBAND. And her all done up in her sister's red lipstick, trying to play at being a grown-up /

LELA. So deep it hurt /

HUSBAND. Like a gash on a doll's face.

LELA. But I thought that it was good. That shudder. I thought that it was good.

Beat.

HUSBAND. So. Here we are.

LELA. It's nice. I like the... I like the sofas.

HUSBAND. The sofas?

LELA. I like the sofas. They're very...

HUSBAND. Comfortable?

LELA. Yes. Very comfortable. Very comfortable sofas.

HUSBAND. You haven't sat on one yet.

She sits on a sofa.

Beat.

Well?

LELA. Very comfortable.

Beat.

HUSBAND. Are you homesick?

LELA. No!

HUSBAND. We're not strictly so far away.

LELA. No I'm not homesick /

HUSBAND. Poor Lela. No time to say goodbye to her parents. No time, even, for a proper wedding.

LELA (*beat*).

HUSBAND. How do you feel about that?

LELA. I don't mind. It was Elle who was always going on about weddings and getting married, not me. She said she was going to have the biggest and most beautiful dress ever, with a dozen petticoats and a five-foot train and a heart-shaped bodice like you've never seen. (*Beat.*) But then she didn't. (*Beat.*) Obviously.

HUSBAND (*beat*).

LELA. And it was exciting, how we drove all night! I've never been this far from... anywhere.

HUSBAND (*beat*).

LELA. And we can always go and visit my family. Won't they be surprised!

HUSBAND (*beat*).

LELA. When are we *actually* going to get married though? Will Elle come? And Jay?

HUSBAND. You have to be careful. Now that you're here.

Beat.

LELA. Why?

HUSBAND. Not so far away, but worlds apart.

LELA (*beat*).

HUSBAND. It isn't a good time. It might be best if you stay indoors for a while.

LELA (*beat*).

HUSBAND. Your people aren't liked much here.

LELA (*beat*).

HUSBAND. Then again, your people don't like my people much.

LELA (*beat*).

HUSBAND. So.

LELA. *I* like you.

HUSBAND. You like me?

LELA (*trying it out*). I love you.

HUSBAND. Do you?

LELA (*beat*).

HUSBAND. Come here then.

Pause.

LELA. Elle had told me all about it of course, and not a better one to tell a girl than Elle. Made it funny, made it silly, made you think of men and what they have to do as sort of lovely and pitiful at the same time. Didn't beat about the bush, either, not Elle, she said that /

HUSBAND. It'll likely hurt like hell, unless you're lucky /

LELA. And it's a hurt you've never felt before. But just to think of other things, things that make you laugh (like how silly it looks between their legs when it engorges, like a tampon in water – that's what she said, like a tampon in water, to make me laugh), and she said that you /

HUSBAND. Just relax and it'll all be over soon /

LELA. She said they're unlikely to take their time about it your first time, if they can help it /

HUSBAND. I'll be gentle.

LELA. And they'll be gentle too /

HUSBAND. Considerate /

LELA. And if it hurts the times after that well, just know that it won't last and soon it'll feel good all over /

HUSBAND. Tender /

LELA. And, remember, there's not much that can be done to a woman's body she can't handle with enough will and hot water, because *that's* in preparation for the big B-I-R-T-H and so /

HUSBAND. If a woman can't take the pain then what's she going to be good for when it comes down to it?

Beat.

LELA. She had a practical side, our Elle. (*Beat.*) And it did hurt. And he did take his time about it. And afterwards, when I had something to compare it to, I learnt that he hadn't been gentle, considerate /

HUSBAND. Tender.

LELA. If the maiden aunts had known that, and hadn't been a hundred miles away back in the mountains and me all alone over the border, well, they would have read the signs and shaken their heads. They would have said, 'Not a good start.' And they would have said, 'A marriage begins as it means to go on.' And they would have said 'Mm-mm-mmmm' and looked at each other and sucked in their cheeks and said no more. But they didn't know, and they were a hundred miles away, and they couldn't read the signs. And I myself couldn't read the signs either, not having the spinster knowledge of sign-reading, but I told myself that like the shudder it was good, and so I closed my eyes and thought of tampons and felt my body revolt /

HUSBAND. The thing about my new wife was that she couldn't get enough of it /

LELA. And I hated it /

HUSBAND. After that first time she wanted it every night, several times a night when I could manage it. In the morning too /

LELA. Which was the worst thing he did, I mean when you think about things in terms of bad worse worst /

HUSBAND. She wanted it whether she wanted it or not /

LELA. Which I don't like to /

HUSBAND. In the arse, in the mouth, in the little cunt on her /

LELA. But the worst thing is to hate something that should
have been /

HUSBAND. Couldn't get enough of it /

LELA. Good.

HUSBAND. Will you shut up? (*Beat*.) Which I had seen in her
from the start, in the bar on the beach /

LELA. The square.

HUSBAND. The beach.

LELA. The square.

HUSBAND. The beach.

LELA. The beach.

HUSBAND. In the bar on the beach. I had seen it in her eyes
over that disgusting drink. I had seen it on her skin. What she
wanted, the potential in her for... I am an observant man.

LELA. He was an observant man, my husband, had a way of
seeing things that were beyond me, and I respected that in
him. You see, it turned out he knew me better than I did,
knew that when I cried I was /

HUSBAND. Just trying to get attention /

LELA. That when I pleaded I was /

HUSBAND. Being manipulative /

LELA. When I asked for something it was

HUSBAND. Greedy, and when she refused me /

LELA. Selfish. (*Beat*.) Yes, I learnt a lot about myself during
those first few months, learnt that, not without a sense of
self-pity I guess, that I was ugly, unlovable, unwanted and
alone, which are, I reckon, the most unhappy things a girl
can be, and yet, I suppose, not a totally unlikely predicament
for many girls to find themselves in if they don't take
precautions. (*Beat*.) Though what those precautions might be
I haven't the foggiest /

HUSBAND. Ugly, unlovable, unwanted and alone /

LELA. Except for him of course, I mean, it must be pointed out, and he was at pains to assure me, that I was alone except for him, unloved and unwanted by anyone but him, ugly to everyone but him, as he was at pains to demonstrate. But, you know, the one thing he tried to teach me that I already knew was that I was ungrateful. Because I had been told since I was a little girl that I was an /

FATHER. Ungrateful dishonourable child! The most ungrateful of all daughters! She ate the icing off the cake, my friends, all the icing off the cake /

LELA. And it turned out I had a lot to be grateful for. Him, for keeping me, when he could have thrown me out on the streets any time he pleased, as he was at pains to let me know, and the streets were dangerous, that I was told too; though of course I didn't need to be told because it wasn't very long before the situation exploded right into the city, right round the corner, beneath our windows, and you could hear it, and you could hear all about it if you cared to listen, even the sound of curfew, could hear the unnatural curfew silence broken all at once by /

Gunfire.

Beat.

But beyond that, it turned out, actually, I was also very grateful to /

JAY. What could be better, I thought, what could possibly be better and more brotherly and more love-erly than to arrange for little Lela's marriage to my old friend, yes, my very established and respectable – not poor either, plenty of hard cash, oh yes – my old friend and business associate, take her off our hands, I thought, take her off her father's hands – make a woman of her. Why not? Yes: this seemed to me to be the absolutely correct thing to do, in my new role of great responsibility as her brother-in-law. And the good hard cash didn't hurt either, I must admit /

LELA. Which is when you realise, suddenly, see more like, all the threads that were already attached to you /

JAY. I bumped into an old friend today, coming back from the bar /

LELA. All the threads pulling tight /

JAY. In the bar, actually, I bumped into him in the bar /

LELA. Who did you bump into in the bar?

JAY. An old friend, a friend from university – now what are the chances of that?

LELA. And so you see, suddenly, like a tapestry, how all along there were threads /

JAY. What, I ask you, are the chances of that? A stroke of luck!

LELA. A real stroke of luck /

JAY. I've arranged for us to meet him for a drink tomorrow, in the evening, a nice little evening drink /

LELA. A stroke of luck or /

JAY. A nightcap. Because I am most keen, oh yes, most keen to introduce you all – and can you imagine? What the chances of that were – ha ha!

LELA. Planned threads and stitches /

JAY. Coming from over the border, after all, as he does /

LELA. Blueprints /

JAY. Tricky place right now, it must be said /

LELA. Where are we meeting?

HUSBAND. It was on the beach.

LELA. Can we go to that café in the square?

JAY. Wherever my little Lela wishes, we can go.

LELA. Threads and stitches, stitches and threads /

HUSBAND. It was on the beach /

LELA. Was it? Was it on the beach?

HUSBAND. It was.

LELA. I don't recall…

JAY. So now please allow me to introduce my very good friend /

LELA. Hello.

HUSBAND. Hello.

They shake hands.

Pause.

LELA (*singing*). 'Oh Western Wind, when wilt thou blow? The small rain down can rain. Christ...'

A MAN (*joining in, singing*). 'Christ, if my love...'

Pause.

LELA. So I lived there with my husband in the flat with the comfortable sofas. And other men came to the flat. They would sit and have a drink, they were his friends. They were polite to me, their eyes went over me and didn't focus. And I liked that, I didn't want anyone to focus on me, because I had developed what I'll call a will to not be seen. Neither seen nor heard. So to creep, very quietly, about the table, like a most talented waiter, one of those waiters with a little moustache and a cloth round their waist like in cartoons who are very servile and very silent, and pour the drink and not be seen or noticed. And being a woman of my family, bird-like as I said /

FATHER. Twitchy, the lot of them /

LELA. Careful movements and gestures; I was good at not being seen /

FATHER. Sneaking, sly, ungrateful /

LELA. And that's a fact. (*Beat.*) I would judge the success of an evening by how few times one of the men had actually glanced at me, a glance was bad, a focused glance was very bad indeed. And the men and my husband would talk, they would talk about the political situation, which if I had been allowed out of the house I'd know was what everyone was talking about not just in our little city but all over the whole wide world, but I wasn't allowed out of the house because it wasn't safe so I would listen to them instead, and they'd talk about who was right and who was wrong and the separatists and the republicanists and the liberationists and the nationalists and the break-up of this and the intervention of that and the refugees coming in and the refugees going out and what was the truth of the matter with the genocides that you heard about trickling on the grapevines like juicy juicy

gobbits of call-to-arms or serves-them-right, and they talked
about my country too, my lovely mountainous, coast-inous
country, and when they talked about it, that I didn't like, not
one bit, because it was when one, if not all, were most
inclined to give me not just a glance but a focused glance
which meant I hadn't done very well that night; but a lot of
the time they talked about business and what was a man in
their position to do about his business and they talked about
the war in the other place and we all knew how good and bad
that had been for business, depending on the business, and
whether we could expect and what we could expect and what
was it we should expect and what was it we were going to do
about it if we were going to do anything at all because what
can one man do in the face of and if I'd had my say I'd have
said yes and what can one woman do in the face of even less I
suppose and meanwhile all this time I would (*Takes a very
stylised tiptoe forward and puts her finger to her mouth.*)
Shhhhhhhhhhhhhhhhhh... And pour the drink. (*Beat.*) And as
for what came next, things unspoken and untold till now,
Lela's story untold in its entirety, / it happened like this...

HUSBAND. It happens like this. I have a wife, my new wife, just
fifteen years old, and she can't get enough of it. Rapacious, is
the word. Sexually rapacious. How can a man, one man, be
expected to satisfy such want in a woman? I have my work, I
have my living to earn – our living now. And meanwhile the
political situation has gone to shit. Us against them, and them
against the other: bombs, bullets and boots. You hear of
mysterious vanishings, impossible genocides, quickly
confirmed or denied by the state media – depending on whose
media and which state. 'Well, so, what more do they want?
They deserve it. Because this is our land.' And that's what we
all say – sheer and total shit. I'll give you my own opinion on
the subject, and it's one that hasn't changed:

LELA (*simultaneously*). This war is bad for business.

HUSBAND (*simultaneously*). This war is bad for business. My
business. Anyone's business. How do you earn a living when
the whole place has gone to shit and you can't get a thing
from here to there or a person to the office without it all
being blown up? Bullets, bombs and boots /

LELA. In the face.

HUSBAND (*beat*). You will understand that I was under a lot of stress at that time. Which is why it is a good thing for a man to have a wife. To help you de-stress /

LELA. In the / face.

HUSBAND. Bad for business. This war is bad for business. But not all business. There are some businesses that war is very good for. These businesses almost invariably involve the recruit, ownership and exchange of other people, in some form or another. This makes sense. People are /

LELA. A valuable commodity /

HUSBAND. And /

LELA. A liquid asset /

HUSBAND. And /

LELA. In the face.

HUSBAND (*beat*). Yes. It is good to have a wife during these stressful times. Because a wife that you love and who loves you is like a home. When you go to her, it is like coming home after a long, hard day's work. (*Beat.*) So. I am a hospitable man. I invite my friends into my home.

Beat.

LELA. It was about this time I started to notice funny things, funny changes, and I knew in my heart that change was *bad*, that little changes were very very bad indeed, and I began to keep an eye out for the little changes that I saw and kept count of them most carefully, I did, and so, for example, exhibit A: more bolts on the front door /

HUSBAND. A man is a king in his castle, and must defend that castle /

LELA. Exhibit B, ladies and gentlemen of the jury: a mattress, one day, in the little back room where I washed the dishes for the eating and the linen for the changing and kept the things for the cleaning of the house /

HUSBAND. You never know, in these times, when you might have an unexpected guest /

LELA. Exhibit C: a gun, one day, of all things, in the drawer of his desk /

HUSBAND. I repeat that a man is a king in his castle /

LELA. And then, exhibit D, note this well ladies and gentlemen of the jury, exhibit D: on the little cupboard, the polished, mahogany cupboard where he kept the passports, his passport and my passport, one day: a lock. (*Beat.*) And no idea, no idea at all, no matter how meticulously I cleaned and cleaned, how I changed the linen, and dishes I washed, could I find the key.

HUSBAND. Why would we need our passports?

LELA. Well, we might want to go somewhere.

HUSBAND. Why would we want to go somewhere?

LELA. Well, you know, we might want to leave, considering the war and all /

HUSBAND. This is my home.

Beat.

LELA. We might want to go on holiday. I've always wanted to go on holiday.

HUSBAND. If we want to go on holiday then I can get the passports myself.

LELA. But how am I supposed to dust inside the cupboard?

HUSBAND. If you go near that cupboard, if I ever see you going near that cupboard for any reason at any time of the day or night I will cut your face. I will take a knife to your face and I will slit your face from lip to ear.

Beat.

LELA. Shortly after that came the time of sleeping in the back room on the mattress amongst the cleaning things, the mop and the dishcloths and the polish and the disinfectant and the scourers and the bleach, because it was now so unsafe for me, considering the war and all and where I had come from and to where I had come, that my husband thought it best that I spent the majority of my time in the back room and only to be let out to cook, and clean the apartment for a couple of hours each day and not even, any more, to serve drinks to the men in the evenings; and not having much to do in the back room, no books to read or pictures to look at or radio to listen to during the times when the radio actually worked and broadcast, well, you could say I was a touch at a loss as to how to occupy myself. But I made do with what I had and spent the majority of my time cleaning the back room and I'm proud to say that whatever happened, whatever happened in that back room I kept it spotless, spotless as a new marble surface like you see in the magazines or spotless as the surface of the lake near my home in the mountains which is like glass, and like glass shuddering like skin when the northern wind licks across it. (*Beat.*) And what happened in that room was this: one night, my husband unlocked the door and showed one of his friends into the room, and his friend looked at me, and my husband didn't, and then my husband went out again and locked the door behind him. (*Beat.*) And then /

FATHER (*bombastically*). Gather round, my friends, and let me tell you the tale of how once, greedy ungrateful girl that she was, my little Lela, the most ungrateful of my three daughters, ate the cake, the whole cake /

LELA. And then he /

FATHER. Her thirteenth birthday cake, the messiah of all birthday cakes that I, her most honourable and distinguished father, had slaved for, yes, slaved for three weeks' wages to buy, yes, buy and bring home this cake. You see it goes like this:

LELA. And so I /

FATHER. Blah blah blah blah blah dishonourable blah blah blah blah thief in the night blah blah blah blah et cetera /

LELA. And it was /

FATHER. A sneaking ungrateful brat blah blah blah icing blah et cetera ha ha ha beat her black and blue /

LELA. And then he /

FATHER. Et cetera et cetera and what have I ever done, my friends, blah blah blah blah ha ha and that's the fact of the matter, so help me God /

LELA. At which point he took me by the hair and smashed my face into the wall so that I was discombobulated and then he turned me over and raped me until I stopped screaming. And then another one came in and did the same. And then another. And then another. My husband had a lot of friends. He's a popular man.

Beat.

FATHER. Ah yes, you remember don't you, my little Lela? She denies it, by God she denies it, but she remembers. Those were the days weren't they, Lela? Ah yes, those were the days my dear...

Pause.

HUSBAND. Unable to support my wife and myself, to pay the bills and put a little something away for a rainy day, I had become stressed and unhappy. I started to lose my hair, my sleep. I was pale. I suffered from erectile disfunction /

LELA. It's true – he did.

HUSBAND. Don't laugh! It's a common condition, and if we want to solve these things we mustn't ridicule them. We have to face them squarely, as a society. For myself, it was easy. It was psychosomatic, there was nothing the matter with me physically. Once I was back on my feet and earning again everything returned to normal /

LELA. And things went from bad to /

HUSBAND. Good. I had a steady income again, tax-free what's more. They say it's the most fulfilling thing a man can do, own and run his own business. Having experienced it, I wouldn't deny that. Small overheads too, in my chosen area. So, yes, all in all bad to /

LELA. Worse. In the beginning was the mattress, and the little supply of condoms which magically replenished itself when I slept, and I serviced one or two clients a night, which was manageable and I had plenty of time to clean up afterwards,

to wash and change the sheet, to pull it tight tight all white
and clean, and to dispose of the condom as though it had not
been – they are such dirty, slimy things; and then it was
several clients a night /

HUSBAND. Better /

LELA. Which made the cleaning afterwards quite a bit harder,
to change the sheets in time I mean, as you can imagine, and
I got very quick at it (quick as my mother actually, who is
particularly quick at sheet-changing having had the
experience of changing sheets for a full household these
thirty-odd years), quick, yes, though concerned about there
not being enough sheets to keep up with it, there not,
perhaps, being enough clean sheets in the world, in the
whole wide world, to change this state to change this state
and then it became many men one right after the other or
even at the same time /

HUSBAND. Best /

LELA. And they'd be in the room waiting and outside the door
lingering in the corridor and so no time no time to clean only
after they'd gone and I had a little just a little so, dripping,
I'd clean and change the sheets and I began to see, strange to
say, threat in the most unlikely things, like orchids. (*Beat.*)
Orchids with their tongues and petal arms. (*Beat.*) And then
it was in the daytime too in the day and no time for changing
or cleaning and the condom supply not often replenished so
much not keeping up with it the success of the business, my
husband's success because it is a fact not universally
acknowledged enough that a man in possession of a good
profit, must be in want of a better one /

HUSBAND. Bested.

Beat.

LELA. I don't know whose she was. My little girl. My lovely
little girl. I don't know. It doesn't matter. Why not all of
theirs? It doesn't matter. She was mine. She nearly killed me
coming out, screaming while I kept mum, screaming in place
of me, tiny little lungs begging life. Life. Life. And outside
only the dead, unnatural curfew silence, split by far explosions

and closer gunfire and the steady fall of bombs bombs bombs; a war child, a war-born child – and that meant something too. (*Beat*.) I know what to do. I sing the songs, a woman's responsibility, I sing the lullaby songs for easing into life and for lulling into sleep.

(*Singing*.) 'Oh Western Wind, when wilt thou blow, the small rain down can rain. Christ / if my…'

A MAN (*taking over, singing*). Christ, if my love were in…'

Short pause.

LELA. I am so. Sick. Of the sound of planes. I wish the war was over.

Planes overhead, bombs drop, explosions.

Silence.

PEACEKEEPER. I've got a condom. I brought one with me. The lads said to, said some of you are diseased. (*Beat*.) I'm not blaming you, I can understand how that would be. Do you understand me? You don't understand me. Here, look, condom. Con-dom. (*Beat*.) It's alright in here isn't it? Not too bad. I've seen worse. What's your name?

LELA (*beat*).

PEACEKEEPER. Your name? Do you understand? (*Pointing*.) You? Name? You?

LELA (*beat*). Your name.

PEACEKEEPER. Hah – no, I don't think so. More than my job's worth, literally. I mean, if this were to get back. We're not allowed, see? It's against regulations, military regulations in general, actually, whores while on duty. You can see why, can't you? – though everyone does of course. You really don't know what I'm saying do you? That's okay. Everyone does it, whores that is. I mean, what else are you supposed to do, trapped in a dump like this? Girls like you, they're all over the place – do you know that? Where did you get those bruises? Did someone do that to you? It's bad to do that. I've seen worse though, since being here. Much worse.

LELA (*beat*).

PEACEKEEPER. What's your name?

LELA. Hah. No. I don't think so.

PEACEKEEPER (*laughing*). Touché. Saw a girl, the other day, didn't have a body for bruising. Eyes like a wild animal. Couldn't do it with her, couldn't bring myself to. Then I refused to pay so they beat her again, heard her screaming. Screamed like an animal, like a fox fucking. (*Beat.*) Won't make that mistake again. Pay up, regardless of the service you do or don't get. Not all of us would. There's some bad ones amongst us, it's fair to say, treat you lot like they'd never treat a girl back home. But there are bad ones everywhere, right? And us, well, we're just normal people too, yeah, just normal men, except with guns. I mean, that's the main difference.

LELA (*beat*).

PEACEKEEPER. It's easy talking to you, like talking to a wall, you girls. It's good to be here, leastways *I* think it is. Some of the lads complain but I think it's a job worth doing, the good thing to do. Obviously it's complicated, I mean, keeping the peace, sure, but under certain conditions a man /

LELA. He sure was a funny one, this boy. Sort of completely immune to what was going on around him – a useful skill that, I should know. I liked him. I liked that he talked though we didn't understand. It was nice to hear words that I didn't understand. I had become sick of words, certain words that I knew too well /

A MAN. Wake! Sleep! Fuck! Clean! Bitch! Whore! Face! Knife! Cunt! Cock! Suck! Fist!

LELA. So yes, there was something refreshing, something even liberating, in words that I did not know.

PEACEKEEPER. Stand up. (*Gestures.*) Up.

LELA (*stands up*).

He looks at her.

PEACEKEEPER. Take your dress off.

LELA (*looks at him*).

PEACEKEEPER (*gesturing*). Your dress, take it off.

LELA (*takes her dress off*).

> *He stares at her.*

> *Beat.*

PEACEKEEPER. You have a waist like a wand. Has anyone ever told you that? Like a wand.

> *Pause.*

LELA. After the war was over, at least technically, there were a lot of foreign people running around keeping the peace and arranging for the the the /

PEACEKEEPER. Transfer of power /

LELA. The transfer of power which is, apparently, a very complicated thing /

PEACEKEEPER. Very complicated. It takes years. Years and years /

LELA. Though why, I don't know /

PEACEKEEPER. Everyone knows, everyone in the world knows that these things take years, and that's why you need what's called an Interim Administration /

LELA. Which is the thing that ensures that the transfer of power happens /

PEACEKEEPER. Peacefully /

LELA. And /

PEACEKEEPER. Democratically /

LELA. Because /

PEACEKEEPER. There is nothing more important in the world than peace and democracy. Which is why we're here, to make sure there's peace and democracy everywhere in the /

LELA. But my husband was very /

HUSBAND. Concerned /

LELA. He was very concerned about /

HUSBAND. How this would affect business /

LELA. The peacekeeping. Though, fortunately, it turned out to be very good for business /

HUSBAND. Very good indeed /

LELA. Lots of new clients /

HUSBAND. Please come in and and make yourselves comfortable /

LELA. They went at it like rabbits, those foreign boys /

HUSBAND. We are so delighted to welcome you to our fledgling country /

LELA. Whatever foreign means in this place. Some of them were good, like my soldier, and some of them were bad, some of them were very very bad indeed, and my husband had to be strict about /

HUSBAND. Not causing damage to the property /

LELA. And lots of money changed hands about this time, I think that the business was expanding, aggressive expansion is the phrase or so I hear; and one day one of them, one of the foreign peacekeepers, brought another girl and she was kept in my little room for two days (which is called a merger and after that we had several mergers), but I didn't really understand what she was saying, this girl, because she was from somewhere else and her language was a little strange, familiar but strange, and she didn't talk much anyway, just cried a lot, and then they took her away again. I don't think she was very well. I remember she wouldn't stop bleeding. I tried to clean her but it hurt her. And I don't think, considering, from taking a look when I was trying to clean her, that whatever had been in her, that it was strictly male. I mean, strictly human. If you see what I mean. (*Beat.*) I have always been very grateful for small mercies.

HUSBAND. Lela & Co. Limited Rules and Regulations, to be strictly followed and adhered to by all parties, associates, clients and employees at penalty of fines, disciplinary action /

LELA. Torture /

HUSBAND. Et cetera et cetera: full discretion on the part of clients and employees to be maintained at all times /

LELA. The first rule of Lela & Co. Limited is you don't talk about Lela & Co. Limited or we'll break your legs /

HUSBAND. This email transmission is strictly confidential and intended solely for the ordinary user of the email address to which it was addressed. If you have received this email in error or are not an intended recipient, please inform Lela & Co. Limited immediately by return of email or telephone and, if advised, delete the email. Failure to do so will result in /

LELA. Us breaking your legs.

HUSBAND. And /

LELA. We'll probably break your legs anyway /

HUSBAND. Full payment on the part of the client is to be made prior to services rendered /

LELA. In cash or we'll break your legs /

HUSBAND. All due respect to the property of Lela & Co. Limited must be employed at all times /

LELA. No cutting or burning, no bruising beyond normal wear and tear, no excessive beating or slapping beyond normal use, no more than two clients to make use of the services of Lela & Co. Limited simultaneously at any one time, no foreign objects outside of the norm to be inserted into the orifices of /

HUSBAND. The company vacuum cleaner /

LELA. With particular penalties laid down for metal and glass, including but not limited to: bottles, poles, gun barrels, knives /

HUSBAND. Any damage to the company vacuum cleaner's orifices, beyond normal wear and tear, will require financial compensation in full at the discretion of the owners of Lela & Co. Limited, as well as repayment in kind /

LELA. We will shove a metal pole up your arse and break your legs and take your money /

HUSBAND. Employees found tampering with the fire alarm /

LELA. The passport cupboard /

HUSBAND. Or stealing company stationery /

LELA. Food or money /

HUSBAND. Will accept the penalty at the discretion of the owners of Lela & Co. Limited /

LELA. I will cut your face. I will take a knife to your face and I will cut your face from lip to ear /

HUSBAND. Thank you for your interest in Lela & Co. Limited. We aim to provide a superior service in all areas. Please feel free to take a feedback form on your way out /

LELA. I do my best I really do /

HUSBAND. Failure on our part to satisfy our clients, where the client has complied in full with the company rules and regulations, will /

LELA. Look /

HUSBAND. You can rest assured, result in a full internal investigation with suitable disciplinary action taken /

LELA. Please /

HUSBAND. We will take your child, Lela, we will take your baby and you will never see her again. You won't know what we did to her, and you will never see her again.

Beat.

LELA. Children are. Dangerous. (*Beat.*) Children are bribes. Children are threats. Children are completely selfish. Their hunger is more important than your hunger. Their pain is more important than your pain. They're noisy, they're noisy and you can't make them be quiet; children will scream if they want to scream even if you baby babble talk even if you coo coo ca choo (*Baby voice.*) 'Please don't scream my little lovely they'll beat me if you scream my little sweet.' Children vomit and shit and you can't keep everything clean. Children are exhausting. Children are more exhausting than being fucked twenty-two times a day. Children break your back and suck

your nipples till they bleed – although grown men do that too.
(*Beat*.) Children. Are dangerous. Children are dependent.
Children are. So small. So very very small. Once my world
was a mountain range. A mountain range with a lake and the
north-north-easterly winds that blew across. And then my
world became smaller and it was just a city, and then it was an
apartment with comfortable sofas, and then a single room with
four walls, and then my world was a mattress. And now. Now.
My world is so small. My world is just the space that I make
with my arms. (*Cradles and bends over her infant*.) So small.
Tiny tiny world. My whole world.

Pause.

PEACEKEEPER. Is it yours?

LELA (*beat*).

PEACEKEEPER. Your baby? (*Mimics cradling a baby*.) Is it
your baby in the other room?

LELA. Yes.

PEACEKEEPER. Who's the father? Better not be me!

LELA (*beat*).

PEACEKEEPER. That was a joke… a… I mean obviously it
couldn't be mine. You don't understand, do you? What's its
name? (*Mimics cradling*.) Baby's name? What's its name?

LELA. Hah. No, I don't think so.

PEACEKEEPER. Hah! You're pretty funny.

LELA (*pleased*). Yes.

PEACEKEEPER. I like coming here. Does that surprise you? I
do. You're the only one I go to now. I like you. Some of the
other places… You couldn't make it up. Ten. Fifteen girls.
Needles on the floor. It's no good, really. No good at all.
Something should be done. To help them I mean.

LELA. Help.

PEACEKEEPER. Yeah, that's right, help. Ahh… I'm just crazy
about your waist. I dream about your waist at night. It's
tiring, what I do, hanging around, arresting people, filling out

forms, looking for unauthorised weapons. There's a hell of a lot of them about I can tell you. At least I don't do mines, there's a thankless job, standing around poking things. People aren't happy either, you think they would be, that you'd be grateful but /

LELA. We'll break your legs.

Beat.

PEACEKEEPER. Right. You do know the weirdest phrases. (*Beat.*) How old are you?

LELA (*beat*).

PEACEKEEPER. How old... Erm...

LELA. Six teens.

PEACEKEEPER. Sixteen? Sixteen! Holy shit! (*Beat.*) How long have you been sixteen for?

LELA (*beat*).

PEACEKEEPER. You really are just a girl. (*Beat.*) But I was only seventeen when I joined up. And I guess if a boy can be expected to put up with that, with the training and that, and the service, then a girl can... I mean... That's not really coming out right. Sorry.

LELA. Sorry.

PEACEKEEPER. No you're not sorry, I'm sorry.

LELA. You are sorry.

Beat.

PEACEKEEPER. This is getting a bit weird. Do you want to... er... They'll be getting suspicious...

LELA. So I had a friend. Lela had a friend. I was very happy with my new friend, I hadn't had a friend for a very long time, not since school really, not since I hadn't seen my sister Elle – but there's more to come on her anyway, as you'll soon hear. But the fact is, I was really happy with my friend, who was, I don't mind saying, *very* handsome, a very handsome, strong soldier with good, warm hands (the aunts would have been pleased) and dirty fingernails (the aunts would not have been pleased but I liked it, I thought it was nice and boyish) and that seemed to make a difference, which it shouldn't, because after a while they all just roll into one anyway or at least that's what you want if you can manage it, but at least, with a handsome, nice young man that you like you can… I don't suppose you could say pleasure exactly. Rather just not mind-numbing devastation. And he seemed quite innocent and cheerful to me and I liked that, like he wasn't able to see… like there was an awful lot he wasn't able to /

PEACEKEEPER. It's nice here I like it here /

LELA. And I liked that he liked it because it made me like it and I wanted so much to make things nice and fresh so that he'd keep on liking it, the way you do with lovers – not that he was a lover I don't mean that, I was faithful to my husband, always completely faithful to him /

PEACEKEEPER. I've got this girlfriend, back home. She's really nice, you'd like her. She sends me stuff, cigarettes and stuff. Which is stupid actually because they're cheaper here anyway but it's the thought that counts /

LELA. What I mean is I wanted things to be nice for my friend. So he'd keep coming back to me. So I managed to make time, somehow you do, and while singing to my little girl I'd scrub the floor as much as possible and I'd wash a shift every night to make sure I had something clean to wear for him and I kept a clean sheet by, which meant I had to suffer sometimes on a filthy sheet many times because I didn't know when he'd turn up but was scared to use up a clean one /

PEACEKEEPER. You remind me of my little sister a bit, sort of neat and tidy. I'm a pig left to my own devices /

LELA. But the problem was I couldn't for the life of me, not for the life of me work out how to source fresh flowers. (*Beat*.) Which is what you do with men that you're expecting, have fresh flowers in the room. I heard it in a song /

PEACEKEEPER. I brought you these flowers. I found them while out on patrol. Wildflowers. They were growing on a dung heap which is a bit gross but I thought they were pretty anyway. Like you. Do you like flowers /

LELA. And the boarded-up window didn't help. Mother always
said what a house needs more than anything else is natural
light and a breeze, says you can't beat it and that's the truth,
and she should know having been a homemaker all those
years and her mother before her and her mother before her
and her mother before her all the way back to the time when
women first started being homemakers and I'm not sure what
they did then, maybe spit-polished mammoth tusks /

PEACEKEEPER. Once when I was little I went to this museum
and there was a mammoth skeleton. It was massive!

Beat.

LELA. But light and air, that I couldn't provide. Which was a
pity really, such a pity, because we didn't have long, he and
I, considering that he wanted to help me, him having made
that clear enough, crystal clear in fact, he'd said it himself,
'Someone should help'. I understood that, I listened very
carefully, and I'd worked hard at school, remember, and not
just geography but everything including my foreign
languages and I knew a little. Actually I was a bit sneaky and
pretended to understand less than I did, although when he
went off on one – he could talk the hind legs off a donkey,
that soldier – I didn't really understand /

PEACEKEEPER. Blah blah blah dishwasher blah blah blah
football yeah it's great blah blah blah Batman and Robin
blah blah blah table leg blah blah blah let's get fucking
wasted blah blah blah selective fire gas-operated assault rifle
blah blah /

LELA. But he didn't mind that, I mean my not understanding –
not my pretending to not understand because he didn't know
I did that so how could he mind it, I ask you? How can you
mind what you don't know? But the fact is once you do
know something, once you know, that's when you mind. And
that's when you do something, right? Once you know
something's bad that's when you stop it, like amputating a
bad leg to stop the poison, to stop the poison to the rest of
the body. To stop the flow.

Pulse.

PEACEKEEPER. It's the first time I've served, I'd only just joined up with the last intervention and I was too young to be deployed and /

LELA. Help.

PEACEKEEPER. Yes help, that's right. I'd have liked to have helped, sure I would, and I won't say I wasn't excited about the thought of going somewhere and er what's the phrase again? Yeah, getting the job done, that's it, the thought of going somewhere and getting the job done and /

LELA. Help.

PEACEKEEPER. Exactly, help. Because you want to help. You hear about all these bad things happening in the world and you think, well, if we can't put a stop to it who can? Because you guys need it, you can't sort it out yourselves because you don't have the the er. What's the word?

LELA. Help.

PEACEKEEPER. Resources, that's it. So it's great to be here doing my bit, I'd never been abroad before actually so that side of it's really exciting too /

LELA. Help me.

PEACEKEEPER. Yeah that's right, help you! That's why I'm here. And I promise you, we're not going to leave till it's all okay again, till the job's done, that's a promise /

LELA. Help me!

PEACEKEEPER (*beat*).

LELA. I'm not. I'm not. I want to go home. I want my mother.

PEACEKEEPER (*beat*).

LELA. I'd planned the speech very carefully, really worked it out to the best of my abilities, racked my brains and my memory for how to get the words in the right order, see? And I was absolutely determined to be calm and cool and collected, not to make a fuss otherwise he'd think I was hysterical and that's the last thing you want when you're soliciting help.

PEACEKEEPER. Yeah, I miss my mum too sometimes, though I wouldn't normally admit it /

LELA. I'm trapped here. I am trapped. I want to go home. Do you understand?

PEACEKEEPER. Okay this is all getting a bit /

LELA. Take me to the governing peace transfer of power body. Take me there, please, and you tell them /

PEACEKEEPER. Whoa okay hold on there /

LELA. You understand, yes? I'm trapped, I'm a trapped girl. Do you understand? My passport is umm no passport. No passport. Help me! Help me! Take me to the governing peace transfer of power body, yes? Yes? You help me!

PEACEKEEPER (*beat*). Okay look, I said – this is really fucked up – I said /

LELA. Help me! Help me!

PEACEKEEPER. Just shut up a second, they'll hear you! (*Looks over his shoulder, grabs her and pushes her down on the floor and lies on top of her, they stay very still. After a silence.*) Listen to me, I told you, you don't understand me do you? But I told you. It's more than my job's worth. Do you know what that means? I help you, I get fired? Yes? Fired?

LELA. He could definitely be a little slow at times, but I had prepared myself for perseverance. What's more, I had the winning hand – just you watch me play it.

PEACEKEEPER. Not fired as in fire argh hot but fire like, you know, when you lose your /

LELA. Lela. My name is Lela.

PEACEKEEPER (*beat*).

LELA. Help me, help Lela. Tell the governing peace transfer of power body that Lela is trapped, you tell them and they help /

PEACEKEEPER. Look Lela – Lela, that's a nice name isn't it? – listen to me, I'm sorry, listen to me, no listen to me, this is really awkward, I mean, I didn't know, I didn't know, yeah? I thought you were okay. And I'm sorry you're not okay, I like you, really I do – do you understand? I like you?

LELA. You like me! Yes!

PEACEKEEPER. Right that's good, yes, I like you. But what I'm trying to say is /

LELA. What I'm trying /

PEACEKEEPER. I'm trying /

LELA. What I'm trying to say is /

PEACEKEEPER. You've got to understand my position, yeah? My position – (*Stops, looks over his shoulder, loudly simulates sex.*) Uh uh uh – I'm a representative of my country, of our military, of the military in general – uh uh uh – You see, it's actually a really big responsibility – uh uh uh uh – if I told them about you, no simpler, I tell my boss – uh uh uh uh… (*Simulates orgasming. Beat.*) I tell my boss you, I get fired. I no job. I disgrace. Our country disgrace. Journalists very tricky. You know journalists? Yes? Journalists break our legs. (*Beat.*) Fuck it. Look. I'm in big trouble. (*Beat.*) No. No help. No. Help.

LELA (*beat*).

PEACEKEEPER. Do you get it? Do you understand? No help.

LELA (*beat*).

PEACEKEEPER. I'm sorry. I really am. I really really am. Very sorry. But there's nothing I can do.

LELA (*beat*).

PEACEKEEPER. Except except except what I'm already doing. And I know, I know it might not feel important, but I promise you it's more important. It's much more important. What I'm doing. And I swear to you, I swear, that I won't leave, not under any circumstances, we won't leave until you're safe and we've got the job. Done.

LELA (*beat*.)

PEACEKEEPER. Because I am prepared to die for this.

LELA (*beat*.)

PEACEKEEPER. So I would appreciate it, actually, if you ever do get out, and I hope you do, really, I'd appreciate it if you wouldn't mention me to anyone because as I said /

LELA (*screams*).

PEACEKEEPER. Are you crazy? Shh! Shh! Be quiet! What are you doing? Be quiet!

LELA *tries to throw him off, then clings to his legs when he attempts to leave.*

LELA. Help me help me help me (*Etc.*) /

PEACEKEEPER. Stop it this is embarrassing let go – It's fine! – Lela shut up they'll come in – Everything's fine in here! No no don't come in /

LELA (*screaming*).

PEACEKEEPER. I didn't do anything look look my hands are clean she just started no don't hit her /

LELA (*howl*).

PEACEKEEPER. Okay look alright back off back off you want money okay here look money look more money take this money – (*Throws fists of money at* LELA, *a hyperbolic amount.*) I'm going fuck me look I'm leaving you're all crazy all of you this whole place this whole look back off I'm going you're all just fucking crazy...

LELA *cries. Eventually:*

LELA. When I explain things to my soldier he's going to understand immediately and he's going to go and get help. He's a little naive, sure, he's a little slow, but he's a good man, a very good man. They tell me not to trust them, the foreigners, they tell me that they're liars, that if they offer me anything I shouldn't take it because it's not true and they're just trying to trick me. They tell me you can't trust a foreigner as far as you can throw him, that's what they say. But I trust my soldier absolutely, yes absolutely. (*Beat.*) You know, I think he's a little keen on me. (*Giggles.*) I know it sounds silly, but why otherwise would he keep coming back, just to me? I think, once he's rescued me and informed the governing peacekeeping transfer of power interim administration body (or whatever it's called) that he might want to marry me, I've just got this feeling, a woman's intuition, as the maiden aunts would say, but I'm sorry to have to reveal – spoiler alert! – I'm just not interested in him in that way. I mean, he's lovely, isn't he? So handsome and sweet-natured. But I don't feel that way about him, and I don't want to go to wherever he's from, I want to go home to my mountains and my mother. So no. I'll have to very graciously decline his generous offer. But we'll stay in touch! That's for sure. We'll write letters and it will help me improve my language skills like you had a foreign penfriend when you were little at school, and I'll tell him what I'm doing and how my little girl's doing, and he'll tell me what he's doing and where he is in the world and who he's helping and we'll be the best of friends forever and ever and maybe one day I'll visit him with my little girl or one day he'll visit me in the mountains and say 'Look how tall she's grown!' and he'll be like an uncle to her, she'll call him uncle, and we'll be happy people for the rest of our lives – three happy people in a very strange world, three happy people, the happiest three people in the world.

Pause.

(*Singing.*) 'Oh Western Wind, when wilt thou blow? The small rain down can rain. Christ, if my love / were in my arms…'

A MAN (*joining in, singing*). 'Were in my arms…'

Pause.

LELA. I service the men. I clean the home. I come out for an hour or so a week and I clean the home and walk around. Walking around is important. It's a form of exercise and a girl needs to keep her calves, that's what Elle always said, a girl needs to keep her calves if it's the last thing she does. (*Beat.*) But then again, Elle said a lot of things. (*Beat.*) I service the men. I clean the home and I walk around and I try and expand my world, to expand it again beyond a mattress and four walls to the size of an apartment and I think, if I can expand it this much, just this much, then I can expand it further to the size of a city and then and then beyond… But no matter how hard I try, I cannot expand my world much further than the space I can make with my arms. (*Beat*.) Once I. Once I. The whole truth and nothing but the truth. (*Beat*.) Once I took my little girl to the bathroom. I had her strapped to the front of my body, slung around at the front of my body as I always did when I cleaned. I cleaned the bath and then I put her in the bath and I turned on the taps and I waited. And I sang her the songs, the songs of sleeping. The mother's songs of sleep. But then I took her out of the bath again and held her and cried because there are some things in life, there have been some things where I have not had the courage of my convictions. I put her in the bath, and I took her out of the bath again and I held her close and I said 'Never never never never.' (*Beat*.) Never. Is a very long word.

Pause.

HUSBAND. After the conflict business was booming and demand was high, what with all the foreigners around. My wife and I were financially stable, and it seemed to me that things could only get better from here. You could begin to rebuild your life in this brave new world. I have only ever wanted to be comfortable, to be secure, to be secure even with the whole world exploding around me. You would not know what it's like to fear for your living, to not know for certain where your livelihood will come from. To learn that you are prepared to do anything, take advantage of any situation to ensure it. There is always a situation to take advantage of. There is always a context. A history /

LELA. I would kill you if I could.

Beat.

HUSBAND. And you have to recognise your place in history. You have to recognise your place in your context, and make what you /

LELA. Listen to me. I would *kill* you if I could.

HUSBAND. Because, really, we're all just alone in the world and it's survival of the /

LELA. Listen to me /

HUSBAND. Fittest /

LELA. All of you listen to me. I don't want you to think that I don't have feelings, because I do. Very powerful feelings that I have, for reasons as yet undisclosed, found ways of /

HUSBAND. And you are either fit, or not fit, fit to survive in an unfair world, or fit only to be swallowed up by it, by the bigger people, the bigger countries. Fit to starve. So, in my position, what's a man to /

LELA. Listen to me. To me. I have found ways of covering of covering up, but not dismantling, no, never dismantling /

HUSBAND. I ask you, in the face of life and all its difficulties, and so many are beyond your control, what is a man to /

LELA. I would kill you if I could /

HUSBAND. It's just. Good. Business.

Beat.

LELA. I would kill all of you. I would take out your eyes and eat them. (*Beat.*) I would eat. Your eyes.

Pulse.

She looks the audience in the eye.

Life has a funny way of throwing luck at you. I know enough now either to think entirely in terms of good luck or bad luck, or, in fact, to do exactly the opposite and not think in terms of luck at all, but just in terms of the things that happen. (*Beat.*) One day I was cleaning the apartment. And on this one day there was no one at home but my husband, not his friends nor his business associates and no mergers at that time, and my husband was in the bathroom reading *The Economist* on the loo, and I was alone. I had my little girl strapped to me, slung across my front, and so I put on my old leather shoes and I unbolted and opened the door and I walked out. I walked out of the door. And I went down the stairs of the apartment block and into the street, and I walked down the street. It was very noisy and very dirty and there were broken buildings and bullet holes in the walls, the walls were like pockmarked faces, like the skin of the city the

whole city was diseased, and all around were foreign police
and soldiers and officials and immigrants and refugees and
homeless and homecoming and there it was this felled city
and these felled peoples and the dust and the dirt – just like I
said – and all this happening all this going on while I had
been cleaning and servicing, cleaning and servicing and
outside the world just turning. (*Beat*.) I have come to know,
over time, something about human bodies, about their smells
and their sounds, their strengths and weaknesses, the
impossible outpouring of bodily fluids, the strangeness of
stray hairs and inexplicable patches of soft on even the most
hardened skin. All this I knew as I walked through the felled
city, and I was lost in the crowded street. And for the first
time in a long time I found a haven in bodies.

Pause.

So I made my way west, following the winds and the transfer
of people – or the winds, perhaps, followed me. In the woods
they have laid down lines that dictate the borders of a
country, and these lines bear little significance to the
demands and formation of the land, and to the demands and
formation of a people, and are, to my mind, spurious to say
the least. But a passport means freedom, the freedom to
move, the freedom to cross the invisible borders laid down
on the land and rearranged at will, at will, yes, but a passport
is the key to the will of men. And in the woods, hidden from
the border crossings and the police and the soldiers who
would hunt them, I saw women and girls flitting between the
trees like deer, trying to find their ways home in dirty clothes
and bleeding feet and cunts and cut-up faces. And there were
places on the road where moving people gathered together to
spend some time in safety in numbers, and did not ask
questions of each other because why would you ask to know
another's story, why ask when what story could you possibly
hear that had any real relevance in the face of bad worse
worst worsted? And there I slept with my little girl on my
chest to stop the men who came to find their comfort in
numbers, and you could hear them sometimes in the night,
seeking their comfort against the comfort of women and girls
who were lost and hidden, and me in the night with my girl
on my chest, and not sleeping properly a wink for fear that I

might, one night, roll over and crush her. (*Beat*.) I do not know when I passed into my beloved country, because the lines of a country are spurious and invisible, but at some point I was there. And then, at some point in this time, I found myself alone again. (*Beat*.) Because you see. You see how it is. I carried her for days, and I let my world be the space between my arms and my body and I sang the songs I did I did but I couldn't I couldn't. There's nothing you can do if the milk stops. And I just. I squeezed and squeezed, squeezed and twisted my breasts but there was nothing left and I was so hungry. And one day she stopped crying. (*Beat*.) I broke my fingernails in the earth on the side of a mountain path and covered her up in the soft wet earth. I knew what to do, a woman's duty, just like I always said. I sang the songs, the songs of mourning and the songs for easing into death, and they caught in the north-north-easterly winds. (*Beat*.) I have walked a hundred miles, I told you so to begin with, did I not? I have come to know something of bodies, and of the body of the land. I know its shifting, and its aesthetic caprices, and its unbelievable indifference to the soft pads of a human being's feet, its indifference to the centuries of line-laying and border-mapping. I have come to know something of a lot of things.

Pause.

And so it came to pass that I came home. I walked into my village and there was much amazement and astonishment and shedding of tears and many happy meetings but not the meeting between me and my grandmother, who had died in the interim, and the maiden aunts had moved up in the world and were sat side by side like Siamese twins in the chair by the stove, and I do not believe that they have left it to this day. And there was much talk on my father's part of how I had eaten the cake and do you remember the cake little Lela, do you remember how and I am tired now of refuting that story so I do not, I nod and I say yes I remember when I ate the three cakes that you had slaved for, my God, seven weeks' wages for seven cakes et cetera et cetera. And they said that the refugees, of which there were many, were a problem but not I to them because I had come home, and that that was all they had wanted, was for me to be home and

safe. (*Beat*.) But then. Perhaps. If I am to be honest, if I am
to be honest and say. The whole truth and nothing but the
truth. Perhaps there was not so much shedding of tears nor so
many happy meetings at my prodigal return, but perhaps, if
I'm going to be honest, which I am, no matter how the words
taste, perhaps there was more, amongst my family and my
village, a sense of. Shame. At my. (*Beat*.) At me. (*Beat*.)
Knowing, as they did, deep in their hearts, knowing what I
did and what I was. And what was done to me. (*Beat*.) And
perhaps, really, they allowed it to be suggested, perhaps it
would have been better for them had I never come back. Had
I tidily died, had I neatly. (*Beat*.) Put away. (*Beat*.) And yes,
in fact, there was not much happiness at all. If I am going to
be honest. No, indeed, no there was not. (*Beat*.) And it so
happened that Jay and Elle came to the village from the city
by the sea, and so we met again at last, and I looked at Jay, I
looked at him and he looked at me and he said 'Such a
tragedy that your husband died in the bombings, such a
tragedy, my dear old friend and business associate; poor little
Lela, but we'll find you another husband, never fear.' And
there was a moment just one moment where things could
have been different where my family took in their thoughts
and their thinkings and looked at me and my body and my
fingernails, the telling signs, and then it came about, it came
down, and they all chorused, 'Yes such a tragedy, poor little
Lela, that her husband died in the war, but you're young yet,
never fear, we'll find you another husband,' and I looked at
Jay and he looked at me and he smiled, convinced now, as he
was and as he had to be, of his own lie, and then I look at
Elle. And she won't look at me. And then I knew. Knew what
she knew. Knew what she had always known, now with her
designer sunglasses no longer fake. And she hasn't looked at
me since and I haven't looked at her, and we will never,
never look at each other, no, never again will our eyes meet.

Pause.

I live now. I am married again, a nice man who doesn't ask
questions, which was, where my family was concerned, a
prerequisite in any partner for me. A proper wedding with
much rejoicing and fuss made and scrubbing of floors and
shelling of peas and the buying of a cake from the French

Patisserie in town and much telling of the tale of how I.
(*Beat*.) Yes well you know that one. It is the story that we tell
in my family. We tell it again and again, we pray it at night
so we don't have to tell the other story. The true story.
(*Beat*.) So I live now. I have one child. He is a lovely boy, a
boy that I love. Now he is older than he was. And now he is
older again than he was before now, and each day he is loved
he is very dearly loved. (*Beat*.) And people say, 'That is
Lela, her husband died in the bombings in the border wars
you know, oh yes, very sad. A widow and so young. But she
has life at least, unlike her poor husband...' to which I bow
my head half-nod half-hung in shame and half... Though
you can't have three halves can you? (*Beat*.) To stop the
words. That could come up. The words that could come up
and say. (*Beat*.) So I live now. And I live in silence and I do
not speak of many things and we do not speak of many
things and the aunts sit in the chair and look sideways and
suck in their cheeks and say 'Mm-mm-mmmm', but those
aren't words and so they're safe, yes safe, there is a safety
for everyone in numbers and in numbers numerous more
numerous than little Lela all alone they have decided silence
and if I were to even, one fine day, say, stand up on the table
and say, 'Lela. My name is Lela, and this is my own story,
this is what happened to me', I have to ask would they even
would they hear because we have a way, a very way, a very
human way of not hearing and not seeing, no not even
seeing, my second husband, the telling marks on me, my
body, no no and so I live now every day I live each day and
so my sister cared for me though she did not care for me and
so my brother-in-law was good though he was not good and
so my husband is dead though he is not dead living now he is
yes and so I had no child though I had a child once and so I
was loved though I was not loved and happy I am me and
my little soldier and my little girl happy yes forever and ever
and so I live now every day no and each day yes and I
promise you I promise you on everything my little son's life
and my little girl's death I promise that this this every day no
this this I swear it I swear. (*Beat*.) This is more than enough.

Pulse.

Slow fade.

(*Singing*.) 'Oh Western Wind, when wilt thou blow? The small rain down can rain. Christ, if my love were in my arms, and I in my bed again.'

Blackout.

End.

A Nick Hern Book

Lela & Co. first published as a paperback original in Great Britain in 2015 by Nick Hern Books Limited, The Glasshouse, 49a Goldhawk Road, London W12 8QP, in association with the Royal Court Theatre, London

Cover image: Root Design

Designed and typeset by Nick Hern Books, London
Printed in Great Britain by CPI Group (UK) Ltd

A CIP catalogue record for this book is available from the British Library

ISBN   978 1 84842 527 9